To Terry Jones

Remember

Kindness

Paddy O'Sul...

Jan. 2011

Love Death and Whiskey
40 Songs
Patrick O'Sullivan

PPP
Published by Patrick Pinder Publisher
Bradford 2010
ISBN: 978-0-9567824-0-3

Cover Photograph
© Zuleika Henry 2010.
The 1987 production of the stage play
Irish Night: the cast sing the title song.

Headlines set in Gotham Medium
Text set in Verlag Light
Book design and typography by Barry Jordan
barry@speardesign.ie   www.speardesign.ie

Love Death and Whiskey

Paul O'Sullivan (signature)

40 Songs
Patrick O'Sullivan

Introduction

A song is like a three legged stool. I am the lyricist, I write the words, and this is my book. So, I will speak first. The song lyric is the first leg of the stool. I am told that there are some people out there who believe that there can be a song without words. Tut.

The second leg of the stool is the music. Writing is mostly a lonely business. So I enjoy the partnership that develops between lyricist and musician. Of course in the beginning of any partnership there is a testing, a sounding out process.

The third leg of the stool is the *performance*. Lyricist and musician, words and music, work towards performance, preferably live performance. We put our work into the hands of the performers. And we bless them.

I love to write songs for a specific performer – more than that, for a special stage presence, for a stage persona. A look, a tone of voice, eyes. I especially like writing for women performers. A song is like a soliloquy in a longer play – there might be, in the background, a longer drama that can be hinted at in the text. For the most part, I honour the dramatic convention that in the soliloquy we hear the truth. The text need not spell everything out, if we know that the performer can inhabit the gaps. In these texts the I is not necessarily me. But I did write all the words.

There are songs in this selection that would not exist if there had not been, waiting for the text, perfect performers for the lyric I had in mind. Obvious examples in this book are *You taught me to cry* and *Irish night.* I suppose that this also means that there are, in my notes or in my head, songs as yet unwritten, waiting for their performers.

It follows from all this that, if this book is to be something more than a collection of one legged stools, you, musicians and singers, must take these lyrics, set them and sing.

This book offers a selection of my song lyrics, written in varying circumstances over many years. Sometimes I was working with musical partners, sometimes I was alone. These are not poems. But it has happened that musicians have taken poems from my table, and have then come back to me to say: Can you please re-write this so that I can set it? And I do re-write. I have allowed some of these more intagliate texts into this selection.

When a number of song lyrics are collected together in one place like this – and not left scattered in guitar cases or on the tops of pianos – patterns and predilections become apparent.

I think that these songs inhabit their own ground. But the traditions, the reference groups, with which the songs connect themselves become obvious. The linked folk traditions of Ireland, Britain and North America. French chanson. Music Hall song. The lyric tradition in English language and literature, with, perhaps, a special bow to Robert Herrick, the master of the very short line.

There is an interest in craft and technique and form. Some musicians, the pop and rock folk, are most comfortable within the verse-verse-middle-eight-verse structure. And it is a good structure – like the sonnet it gives a place where the thought must turn, the *volta*. Some musicians prefer the crafted form of the literary lyric. Other musicians like a less strict form – their music likes something that the music must rescue, or their music likes to impose its own will on the text. Some musicians like a clean and fragrant line, others like jagged edges. I am easygoing about all this. I like to hear my songs sung.

A song lyric is made up of words, words have meanings, and songs have subject matter. There is, in these songs, an interest in what might be called the traditional, or even the familiar, subject matter of song. There is also an interest in taking song into unfamiliar territory. There is no fear of difficulty and experience, emotion and, indeed, sentiment. I give the musicians and the performers something to work with.

There is, you will see, a certain tenderness towards songs built around the names of places – though I have, wisely I think, rationed these in this selection. I have included some songs written for stage plays, where the analogy with the soliloquy becomes more than an analogy.

This book, a selection of my song lyrics, is dedicated to the musicians and performers I have worked with. It is offered to them with my thanks.

Patrick O'Sullivan
Narrowboat *June*
October 2010

The Songs

9

Assignations

Assignations in crowded places,
searching for you in a sea of faces,
covert kisses, quick embraces...
I'd rather be lonely.

Conversation comes in snatches,
steers around the sticky patches.
My souvenir, a book of matches...
I'd rather be lonely.

      Real lovers talk in future tenses,
      hope, and promise recompenses.
      We drink white wine, on the rocks.
      Hand in hand, we watch the clocks.

All day I wait for you to phone me.
You say, Who knows what might have been if only...
I never thought I'd rather be lonely...
But...
I'd rather be lonely.

Clover the kitten

Clover helped me write this song.
She sits perched upon my shoulder,
bites my ear when I go wrong:
such a sense of time has Clover.

If I'm stuck this cat descends
to the jungle on my table.
There she stalks and hunts my pens
round the phone and down the cable.

Meanwhile I do much the same,
hunting words and shades of meaning
through the jungle of my brain
to some bright and happy clearing.

So, each does what each is best at
in the world to make it brighter.
Clover is the cleverest cat.
I'm the poor, hard-working writer.

Love, only hold me

Love, only hold me,
don't fear my tears.
Remember you told me
of your crying years.

Give me your shoulder
to bury my face,
wiser and older
and used to disgrace.

Yes, you can chide me,
poor little waif,
as long as you hide me
and let me feel safe.

Just let me shiver
and clutch your lapel,
now and forever,
all will be well.

Safe harbour

This time last night
what were we?
Two ships adrift
on a troubled sea,
little knowing
we would be
     in safe harbour,
     safe harbour, today.

This time last night
each showed each
the wrecking surf
along the beach,
not believing
we could reach
     safe harbour,
     safe harbour, today

     Glass falling, storm warning,
     small boats seek the bay,
     safe harbour in the morning,
     safe harbour today.

This time last night
we were lost,
storm crazy,
star crossed.
Together find
what we need most,
     safe harbour,
     safe harbour, today.

The gauntlet

Do not expect too much of grief:
it will not question or confirm belief,
it will not slam the door to doubt,
not lock it in, nor keep it out,

it will not orient the heart
with whispers from a place apart,
nor will it let the silence grow
until we know we do not know,

it will not sleep, nor offer rest,
it will not satisfy a quest,
and, so much milk and water spilt,
it will not hone or temper guilt.

The iron hand discards its glove:
we would not grieve did we not love.

Deserve my love

Deserve my love,
only deserve my love.
Save love, serve love,
let love be magnificent.
Only deserve my love.

Do not shame my love,
do not shame my love.
Blame me, shame me,
let me seem the innocent.
but do not shame my love.

My love,
the light in your eyes,
the strength of your arm,
my love overcame me.
My love,
the hurt of your lies,
the unthinking harm.
Would you let my love shame me?

Let me sing my love,
let me sing of my love,
sing proudly, sing aloud,
innocent, magnificent.
Let me sing my love.

Written for the stage play, *Dear Maria*. Two women married to useless men. In the liminal place of this quiet song the audience learns that the women are not fools – but are simply in love.

The plains of Mayo

In the spring, when days grow longer,
I will rise and I will go,
my pledge I will not linger
till I reach County Mayo.

In Balla you will see me dancing.
I'll sing the song I know the best,
and any song that takes your fancy.
In Kiltimagh I'll take my rest.

It is as if the warm sun rises
and all the mists of sadness go
when I think of fair Claremorris
and all the wide plains of Mayo.

There I will be with my own people,
there in Mayo, on the plain,
then the years will surely leave me.
I will be glad and young again.

Written for the
stage play, *Irish
Night*. With homage
to Anthony Raftery
'Anois teacht an
Earraigh' – 'Spring
is now coming'

The last train

O the last train
is a slow train,
it meanders
through the night.
It's the milk train,
it's the mail train,
and it stops at
every light.

It is loaded,
it is crowded.
I'll be riding
in the van,
I'll be sitting
on my suitcase.
I'll be talking
to the man.
As the night goes
even colder
I'll be sleeping
when I can.

I'll be dreaming
of the morning
when the sun comes
on the right.
I'll be thinking
of you waiting,
waiting for me
through the night.

I will lean
against the window,
I'll be counting
sheep and farms.
I'll be longing
for the morning
when I'll hold you
in my arms.

Irish night

I awoke one Irish night
and listened to the stream.
I lay awake one Irish night,
still troubled by a dream.

I left home one Irish night:
the sky was full of jewels,
the moon and stars were shining bright
and silvering the ruins.

> Chase a star,
> hunt moonbeams:
> my Irish night was full of London dreams.

My mother never looked at stars,
I'm far too busy now.
And if my father looked at stars
he only saw the plough.

Somewhere surely one bright star
by right belongs to me.
One Irish night I saw my star
shine across the sea.

> Chase a star,
> hunt moonbeams:
> my Irish night was full of London dreams.

The title song for the
stage play, *Irish Night*.
And it does what a title
song should do.

Just irrigation

I never understood her tears.
I tried, as best I could,
to still her sadness, calm her fears:
it didn't do much good.

She'd smile and simply pat my hand
and give no explanation:
you don't need to understand,
it's just, just irrigation.

Just irrigation,
tears must flow,
just irrigation,
love will grow,
just irrigation,
tears must fall,
just irrigation.

There are many feelings words can't catch
though words still have to try.
As I was puzzled by her words
you're puzzled when I cry.

Though now I think I understand
I can give no explanation
and I must simply pat your hand
and say, it's irrigation.

Just irrigation,
tears must flow,
just irrigation,
love will grow,
just irrigation,
tears must fall,
just irrigation.

In my heart

In my heart a tender feeling,
I never thought I'd find it there,
something like a wish or promise,
something very like a prayer.

Walk with me and stay beside me
from this moment, ever more.
Let me have your love to guide me,
like a beacon on the shore.

In my time of desperation
let me only look to you
to find hope and consolation,
heart that's strong and love that's true.

I think this life is like a journey
and we are pilgrims on the road,
clasping hands at every turning,
share the task and share the load.

I can face the mountain ranges,
all the tempests of the sea,
I can stand the seasons' changes
since I know that you're with me.

Back to him...

And so leave the bed,
put on your clothes.
When everything's said
everything goes,
     as you will,
     back to him,
     back to him.

He gave you years,
we've had our days,
and after the tears
everything stays
     as it was,
     back to him
     back to him

I gave you magic.
He waits in your home,
sure and lethargic,
he knows you will come,
     and you do,
     back to him
     back to him

And we won't know if what we have
was worth the building on,
and you will be just one more ghost
when you're gone, when you're gone.

And so out the door,
down to your car:
you learnt once before
you're safe where you are,
     as you were,
     back to him,
     back to him.

Midnight telephoner

Dear love, dear loner,
a lot like me,
midnight telephoner,
far across the sea,
you feel lost, you feel lonely,
you have nothing to say,
of course, of course, you phone me,
only an ocean away...
only an ocean away...

Across the canyons of the deep
the transatlantic cables leap;
while half the world is still asleep
they bring me promises to keep,
dear love,
only an ocean away...

Throughout the ocean in between,
the haunt of whale and submarine,
so many voices sing and keen
of what once was or might have been,
dear love,
only an ocean away...

You know I never tell you lies,
I promise you the sun will rise:
it pays the moon to advertise
like neon in the night time skies,
dear love,
only an ocean away.

The finest town in Lancashire is Bolton

The finest town in Lancashire is Bolton.
Go there,
knock on any door,
say I sent you.
The folk of Lancashire,
will not make me a liar.
They will take your hand,
invite you in,
and sit you by the fire...
and the finest town in Lancashire is Bolton.

The warmest town in Lancashire is Bolton,
a working town,
smokey.
Smoke won't hurt you.
As if smoke could ever harm,
that certain smokey charm
of Bolton folk, so welcoming, hospitable and warm.
The finest town in Lancashire is Bolton.

There are some think well of Bury,
but I see no need to worry.
And some make claims for Wigan.
I wouldn't know where to begin.
So I'll keep it plain and simple,
for I see you're in a hurry:
the finest town in Lancashire is Bolton.

Written for the stage
play, *Dear Maria*. This
song marks the end of
Act 3, and the end of the
play. Very music hall.

Angel in the gallery

Forget your duchesses,
noble dames and such as as
sit in their stalls and boxes es
in their silken frocks es es,

with all their airs and graces es
and their painted faces es.
See me flee their clutches es:
o yes, forget your duchesses.

> For the girl that I love
> is as pale as a dove,
> and she sits, far above,
> like an angel in the gallery.

> I need just raise my eyes
> to behold paradise,
> there she is, chaste and wise,
> my angel in the gallery.

Though I may seem a bit of a fop
My love isn't one of your nobs,
by day she works in a shop,
but at night she sits in the gods

> When such love makes us strong
> we can all sing along
> and dedicate my song
> to the angel in the gallery.

One of the music hall songs
written for the stage play,
Semper Bella. The first two
verses have to be sung with a
stutter. I know it's hard.

If you left him

If you left him would he know,
would he notice, would he care?
Would he notice you had gone
when he hardly knows you're there?

What's the point of hanging on
in hopes that things will change?
You're not lovers any more,
just strangers being strange.

I think you know you've given him
everything you have to give,
and somewhere, waiting patiently,
your own life's there to live.

I suppose you once meant much to him
though he finds that hard to show.
Now your devotion only means
he never needs to grow.

If you left him would you go
in autumn or in spring,
the evening or the morning time,
and would you start to sing?

Or weeping for dishonoured time
would you seek time to grieve?
Or is it that you've kept yourself
from knowing you can leave?

Irontown

I live alone in Irontown
where forge and furnace blaze.
The yellow rust has stained the town:
it stands but it decays.

The yellow forges in the night,
they burn like captive stars.
But here we don't know day from night
and measure time in years.

I give my life to Irontown,
to bayonets and to guns.
The yellow rust has stained my blood:
it runs red when it runs.

My eyes are iron-encrusted now,
my hearty is iron-bound.
I know that it would break my heart
if I but look around.

I live alone in Irontown,
a life I cannot share.
With so much life to iron pledged
I have no life to spare.

And if I left these iron lands
to what land would I go?
What other work would earn my bread
when iron is all I know?

Kissed on the meridian

We walked in the park
as far as the sign
where the earth is divided
by an imaginary line –
I tell you this because

> I was kissed on the meridian:
> he gave the world a shove,
> two hemispheres spun faster
> and I fell, in love.

The transatlantic tourists
and the frail Japanese
their cameras clicked
amazed by sights like these.
But I didn't care.

> I was kissed on the meridian:
> he gave the world a shove,
> two hemispheres spun faster
> and I fell, in love.

I am told that in Samoa,
on the other side of the world,
because of this line,
the people are confused, they
don't know if it's Monday or it's Tuesday.
I feel fine.
Though it is true that

> I was kissed on the meridian:
> he gave the world a shove,
> two hemispheres spun faster
> and I fell, in love.

The longest night

My love, when we two meet again
the winter will be just half done,
the snow piled in the street again,
the pavement never brightened by the sun.

I will be cold and cheerless then
but do my best to play my part:
you must be bold and fearless then,
you know the way to warm my heart,

> The sun so far away,
> so cold, and hid from sight:
> my love, the shortest day,
> but O
> the longest night.

Outside the wind will roar again,
outside the streets will fill with gloom;
inside our spirits soar again,
we make a tropic island of our room.

A time for interlacing then,
the bitter cold of winter gone;
a time for warm embracing then,
and safe until the distant dawn.

> The sun so far away,
> so cold, and hid from sight:
> my love, the shortest day,
> but O
> the longest night.

To be Irish

You don't know you're Irish
till you're Irish no more,
you don't know you're Irish
till you walk out the door
and carry your suitcase
to some foreign shore:
so is this what it means
to be Irish?

A son or a daughter,
that's how you were known,
the child of your father,
your mother's dear son.
You were never uncounted
and never alone:
you didn't know what it meant
to be Irish.

You lived in the house
at the head of the glen,
you walked to the chapel
as one of the men.
You stood in the doorway
then walked back again:
it was easy enough
to be Irish.

You don't know you're Irish
till your Ireland is gone,
hull down in the mist of
a soft Irish dawn,
held down in the mist of
a memory half gone:
tell me, what's it like
to be Irish?

This song was
written for the
stage play,
Irish Night.

Weary Angel
(an epithalamion)

I say an angel stands beside us now,
a weary angel, longing for his bed.
With trembling hand he mops his fevered brow,
and says, At last I've got them safely wed.

The other angels stand around and cheer.
They never thought he'd do it, but he did.
In heaven now they're breaking out the beer,
and singing, Here's looking at you, kid.

But our particular angel,
his feathers all in a sweat,
says, Hold on, lads,
I can't get drunk,
cause they might need me yet.

When he took on this job he took a hard one,
he took a job that no one else could do.
O go and get your pint, our weary guardian.
We'll manage for the moment without you.

With trembling hand he reaches for his Bass,
and with a crumpled feather mops his brow,
and with a certain pride he downs his glass:
a weary angel stands beside us now.

I dreamt you came to me

I dreamt you came to me last night
as though you'd never gone;
you came in darkness, softly, lest
you wake me from my dream;
but I, to catch the morning light,
had left the curtains drawn:
a silver statue, you undressed
and came into my arms.

Came into my arms...

And, lover, you were not surprised
to meet my waiting arms;
you knew that I'd pretended sleep,
you laughed, and kissed my face:
and then my flooded heart with joy
awoke me from that dream
to misery made worse by hope
and nothing in your place.

Nothing in your place...

And if I sleep and dream again
that you come in the night
I must be firm, but I'll be kind,
I'll speak to that dream you,
I'll tell that dream that you have gone
and that it isn't right
of dreams to come and haunt my mind
and trouble me with joy.

Trouble me with joy...

The flowers of the forest

Dawn is the time
to rise and go faring,
days are for work
to earn our daily bread,
dusk is return
tired and near past caring
to wearily find
a pillow for the head.

    We live for a while
    like the flowers of the forest,
    the flowers of the forest
    that bloom and fade away.
    Though we can't live for ever
    we can live good and honest
    and dance in the sunshine
    of our one bright day.

There is still time for song
at the end of the evening,
there is still time for song
in the darkness of the night,
there is still time for singing
at parting and grieving
in the hope we will meet again
in a new day's light.

    We live for a while
    like the flowers of the forest,
    the flowers of the forest
    that bloom and fade away.
    Though we can't live for ever
    we can live good and honest
    and dance in the sunshine
    of our one bright day.

Written as a wake
song for the stage
play, *Irish Night*.

The green hills of Australia

When I wake up in the morning I lie in my bed
and I pause for fear of losing the dreams in my head,
for over the factory, and over the sea
the green hills of Australia are calling to me.

The green hills of Australia that I see in my mind,
in a fold of the mountains, are gentle and kind.
In a fold of the mountains, in an arm of the sea
the green hills of Australia are calling to me.

I will wander in the morning, bare feet on the grass,
I will gather arms of daffodils from the fields as I pass,
I'll look over the mountains and over the sea
at the green hills of Australia, still calling to me.

Lilly's Special Verse:

I will pack up by trousseau, I will pack up my kit.
Like Robinson Crusoe, on my island I'll sit,
until my Man Friday climbs out of the sea.
The green hills of Australia are calling to me.

Written for the stage play, *Dear Maria*.
The three Doorley sisters dream of
a better life. The Australia of their
imaginations is very like Ireland.

That old song again

Outside the trees are greening
and singing in the breeze.
Inside my heart they're echoing
and stirring memories.
My heart once knew as sweet a song
as sung by wind in trees.
And I hear someone singing
that old song again,
  I hear someone singing
   that old song again.

I stand behind my window,
I watch the clouds sail by.
Sometimes the clouds must bear too much,
I've often seen them cry.
Today they sing a different tune,
today they're bright and high.
and I hear someone singing
that old song again,
  I hear someone singing
   that old song again.

  That song was meant for two to sing
  and can't be sung by one,
  was meant for me and you to sing
  and finish, once begun.

Outside the birds are singing
and flying round in pairs.
What secrets can the songbirds have
that give themselves such airs?
Some secret that I share with them
for, taken unawares,
I can hear me singing
that old song again,
  I can hear me singing
   that old song again.

The Prince
of Clouds

He gave a brilliant lecture
on the social life of clouds,
how some live isolated
and some collect in crowds,

how some clouds cling together
and mingle in the heights,
and others clash with lightening flash
and thunder in the night.

And after, over coffee,
I watched his calm blue eyes
and wondered how he came to know
so much about the skies.

Just then a foreign stranger
came up to him and bowed:
at last I see this man must be
the famous Prince of Clouds.

The Prince of Clouds, soaring,
the Prince of Clouds, sailing,
the Prince of Clouds, floating,
between the sky and the sun.

The Prince of Clouds, searching,
the Prince of Clouds, seeking,
the Prince of Clouds, questing,
where no one else had gone.

And, yes, I heard him lecture,
I heard every word he said.
That's how he works like you and me
to gain his daily bread.

I thought he did it very well,
not humble or too proud:
he earned his fee with dignity,
the exiled Prince of Clouds.

Who lost the most

It was only an elegant party
and I thought I might stay for a while
when I see you still hale and still hearty
and still with that confident smile.

We meet like old comrades in wartime
with a cry and affectionate hug
and soon start to talk about our time
and who lost the most by our love.

We were always a civilised couple,
of course we decide we must meet,
you'll buy me a drink or a double
and I'll cook you something to eat.

We dine by the light of one candle,
you pour out rough wine from a jug,
and all we can do is to wrangle
about who lost the most by our love.

And if one thing then leads to another
it's only because we're old friends
and I, for one, never could bother
to untangle your means from your ends,

and if after I flop down beside you
to share one last smoke on the rug
it shows no one knows more than I do
who it was lost the most by our love.

Young men in winter, old men in spring

Young men in winter,
old men in spring,
young men in winter,
old men in spring.

It may seem to make no sense whatever,
and I try to explain it again,
why I take only young men in winter
and save up the spring for old men,
and, though it's my choice, I admit it,
I question my choice now and then.

For in winter I need conversation
and young men, they don't know a thing.
In spring I want music and passion
and old men get tired and can't sing.
But I follow my first inclination
and welcome the old men in spring

Young men in winter,
old men in spring,
young men in winter,
old men in spring.

For young men are sweeter and stronger
and warmer in winter's cold sting,
and old men have charm and take longer
and are grateful to get one last fling.
And it is right, one more winter over,
to be kind to the old men in spring.

Young men in winter,
old men in spring,
young men in winter,
old men in spring.

Autobiography of a navvy

There's no great wisdom in the song I sing,
but I know enough to know this one thing:
a man's no man unless he can work
and there's no work for a man in County Cork.

I kissed my mother and put on my coat,
I went to Dublin and got on the boat.
Now I know enough to know I'm a fool,
for I ended up on the lump in Liverpool.

    In a greasy café I buy my grub,
    my friends I buy with a drink in a pub.
    Like a pick and shovel I am bought and sold,
    I'm the subby's man and I am not my own.

I miss my family, but we're not in touch,
I pray too little and I drink too much.
My face is bold, but my heart is cold,
and who will care for me when I am old?

I think the Irish are a cursed race,
I think they'll vanish and not leave a trace.
From east to west and from pole to pole
they work on every man's land, but not their own.

The title pays homage
to Patrick MacGill. One
of the songs used in the
stage play *Irish Night*.

You taught me to cry

I had so much to learn
when I met you,
fresh from the country,
like milk and eggs,
innocent eyes
of forget-me-not blue,
tangled hair
and coltish legs.

And you were so wise
in the ways of the world,
you took me in hand,
you guided my style,
the way my hair curled,
the clothes I should buy.
You taught me to love,
and you taught me to cry.

You taught me to cry,
you taught me to cry,
I had so much to learn,
and you taught me to cry.

I can order in French
and get what I want,
I can talk of the wine
of the Rhine and the Rhone,
the sun on the isles,
the snow in Vermont.
I can travel the world,
but I travel alone.

You showed me the world,
I saw through your eyes
what was in good taste
and what to despise.
How should I judge you,
my standards so high?
I had so much to learn,
and you taught me to cry.

> You taught me to cry,
> you taught me to cry,
> you taught me to love,
> and you taught me to cry.

The crumble song

He bakes a good crumble
for someone he loves,
of apple and honey
and scented with cloves.
He makes a good ballad
to tell of this feat,
as fine as the crumble
and almost as sweet.

And he sings that song out of key...
All this he has done for me.

He spreads a good table
and sits at the head.
He likes to see friends there
and to see his friends fed.
He tells a good story,
crouched over his ale,
a long shaggy dog
with a sting in the tail.

And no one laughs louder than he...
All this he has done for me.

And yet he is quiet and humble,
though he has every right to be proud,
and - here is the cream on the crumble -
he loves me and says it out loud.

Bright flowers spring up
at his word of command,
and apple trees bend
to put fruit in his hand.
The beasts of the field
and the birds of the air,
they gather around him
to join him in prayer.

And he makes a really nice cup of tea...
All this he has done for me.

They have closed the border

They have closed the border,
I cannot get through.
I will stand by the wire
and hope to see you.

If you stand on that hill, love,
and if you wear blue
I will stand by the wire
and know I see you.

    Do not wave, do not sign,
    do not show you are mine,
    for who knows who will watch and will see?
    You must stand, and stand still,
    your blue gown on that hill,
    and no one will know you but me.

They have closed the border,
they have shackled the gate.
Who gave the order
decided our fate.

The men in the tower
stand early and late.
They have closed the border,
I will stand here and wait.

Do not wave, do not sign,
do not show you are mine
for who knows who will watch and will see?
You must stand, and stand still,
your blue gown on that hill,
and no one will know you but me.

I will stand by the wire,
the barb on my cheek.
I will stand by the wire
cold blooded and meek.

They have closed the border,
I cannot get through.
I will stand by the wire
and pray I see you.

I met my love in Baltimore

I met my love in Baltimore
behind the greyhound station.
He changed a banknote for the phone,
I changed his destination.

We went south cross Carolina,
cause he'd never been there,
took a fancy to Savannah,
saw the new year in there.

All journeys deviate:
you may think your road is straight,
but you learn, and learn too late,
I never meant to be here.

There was work in Louisiana:
we pulled on our new blue jeans,
bought a postcard of Savannah
to show in New Orleans.

There we listened to the jazzmen,
arm in arm in Jackson Square,
far too happy to examine
the chance that took us there.

    All journeys deviate:
    you may think your road is straight,
    but you learn, and learn too late,
    I never meant to be here.

I don't mind the south in summer
but I like to see the autumn;
saw two tickets for New Hampshire.
Like a fool I bought them.

He called me a rootless drifter.
I said he was stuck in mud.
Further argument came swifter,
too much harm for little good.

    All journeys deviate:
    you may think your road is straight,
    but you learn, and learn too late,
    I never meant to be here.

Shabby dress

And in the evening, home from work,
I take my key and climb the stair,
and find her waiting in the dark,
so still I hardly know she's there,

but meeting her is no surprise,
I know her well, her sad grey eyes,
her long brown hair, her shabby dress.
I say, hello, my loneliness.

I push the door and let her in,
and pour myself an evening drink.
The empty bottles in the bin,
the dirty dishes in the sink,

they do not move, they do not stir,
yet everything is touched by her.
Her sad grey eyes, her shabby dress,
I contemplate my loneliness.

Written in homage
to *La Solitude*,
paroles et musique
par Barbara.

My loneliness, she likes the nights,
she likes to sit beneath the stars,
too shy to come out to the lights
and meet my friends in public bars,

and they don't like to hear her named,
and truthfully I am ashamed,
ashamed of her, her shabby dress,
her sad grey eyes, my loneliness.

But she, she doesn't seem to mind,
she never comments anyhow,
but patiently and always kind
she settles down beside me now,

and she will spend the evening there,
just watching through her long brown hair.
Her sad grey eyes, her shabby dress,
I'm used to her, my loneliness.

Sunflowers

I went back to the old place yesterday,
just to show myself I could.
It wasn't far to drive out of my way,
and the roads were always good.

The cottage looked ramshackle, overgrown,
the garden gone to seed,
with everything we'd planted overthrown,
and every flower a weed.

I peered through grimy windows. Did I think
I'd see you still in there,
rinsing out paint brushes at the sink,
the lamplight in your hair?

And then I turned a corner. There they were,
the sunflowers, standing in a line,
and for a fragile moment in the air
the scent of oil and turpentine.

You always painted sunflowers. Sunflowers
were your image of the earth.
They have a true philosophy. They love
the sun that gave them birth.

You always painted sunflowers, towering
above your brown and naked child.
We lived amongst the sunflowers, flowering
on your canvas, growing wild.

You always painted sunflowers, gleaming
the way you said that only sunflowers do.
I never understood the sunflowers' meaning
or understood what sunflowers meant to you.

I went back to the old place yesterday,
and I thought you'd like to know
whatever might have come and come what may
the sunflowers grow...
the sunflowers grow...
the sunflowers grow...

Tooting Bec

I lost my heart in Tooting Bec.
I stood amazed and fearful,
for there she kissed me on the neck
and whispered in my earhole.

O, those southern girls,
so hot blooded.

I must go back to Walworth now,
to mum and dad and brother,
and I must find the nerve somehow
to tell them that I love her.

My dad will snort behind his paper,
my little brother snigger,
but what I say is, soon or later,
he'll know better when he's bigger.

My mum will put her knitting down –
she's always knitting new things –
and all she'll say is, listen son,
they're funny folk in Tooting.

O is it that hot southern sun,
that melts the very tarmac,
that makes the blood of Tooting run
so passionate and ardent?

Or is it that the southern stars
have power beyond the normal,
while we in Walworth live our lives
so strait-laced and so formal?

O she is like the southern sun
that burns from May to August,
and she is like that southern sun
that burns as fierce as sawdust.

And when she touches me I burn
as bright, as hot as she does.
and as I travel north I yearn
to travel south to see her.

O those southern girls,
so hot blooded.

In Madrid

You ask me where I am going:
if I told you you'd not let me go.
You ask me my reason for travel:
the truth is I'm not sure I know.

But I know there's a fair southern country
whose people cry out to be free.
They have called on the world to come help them,
and I know that the world includes me.

So I go, as I must,
to Madrid,
to drink or to fight,
to love or be lonely,
to live or to die
in Madrid.

You notice I carry no baggage:
I live on whatever I find,
and I look for a way of discarding
the baggage I have in my mind.

In the end this time calls for action,
and leaving such baggage behind,
and putting your mouth where your heart is,
and putting your heart on the line.

So I go, as I must,
to Madrid,
to drink or to fight,
to love or be lonely,
to live or to die
in Madrid.

That man in the heat of the battle
played a brave and responsible part;
near the University quarter
he fell, a shot through the heart.

His comrades recovered the body
and carried him down to the square,
and gathered a posy of flowers,
for they knew, everyone that was there,

they had come, as they must
to Madrid,
to drink or to fight,
to love or be lonely,
to live or to die
in Madrid.

The mermaid and the drunks

The mermaid came out of the river
where the river reaches the sea;
she paused on the strand to stand and shiver
and brush the sand from her knee.

Naked, the sea king's daughter
stood on the moonlit sand;
she had come from that kingdom under the water
to see how they live on the land.

> The drunks in the bar by the harbour
> were singing
> of Mollie and Jeannie,
> were singing
> of Nellie and Ann:
> the mermaid, enticed to that bright neon arbour,
> entered the kingdom of man.

The drunks were amazed by this vision.
They ceased their drinking and lies,
and then, with a scowl, and a howl of derision,
refused to credit their eyes.

This song is a version
of Pablo Neruda,
*Fabula de la sirena y
los borrachos*

They threw corks
and bottle tops,
they spat
and screamed in her face.
They burnt her
with the butts of cigarettes.
They leant on a good pal's shoulder
and shuddered with glee.

Heart that had never known fear did not sigh,
eye that had never known tear did not cry.

> Heart that had never known fear did not sigh,
> eye that had never known tear did not cry.

The mermaid looked at the drinkers,
she studied each wrinkled face,
and, bemused by this college of scholars and thinkers,
returned to the ocean and peace.

And the drunks, they drank something rotten,
and slept, their aim from the first.
At a loss to recall what it was they'd forgotten
they woke to headaches and thirst.

Barbara, remember

Barbara, remember:
it rained all day.
I walked round the town
and lost my way.
Two hours to kill
before my train,
and the rain came down,
the happy rain.

And you ran through the rain, Barbara,
laughing eyes and wet hair,
and your tall man stood waiting
in a sheltered door,
and he called out your name, Barbara,
he called out your name,
and you ran to his arms, Barbara,
you ran through the rain.

Barbara, remember:
he held you close
and put his hands
round your merry face,
and he said your name,
and kissed your mouth:
all this I saw
and I loved you both.

I hope you don't mind that, Barbara,
but I loved you then
for your bright merry face
and your tall loving man,
and I wished you well, Barbara,
o I wished you well,
as you stood there together
and the good rain fell.

'Rappelle-toi Barbara':
this song is a version
of Jacques Prévert's
poem, *Barbara*.

Barbara, I remember:
the rain came down,
I walked round the streets
of that little town.
You and your man
in the wet cobbled street,
and I happened by
and saw you meet.

I saw you that once, Barbara,
and only that once,
and I wonder what life
has done to you since,
for life can be stupid, Barbara,
as maybe you know,
but I hope, o I hope, Barbara
but I hope that life's been good to you.

There was so much in you then, Barbara,
so much goodness and laughter,
I know you lived well,
whatever came after,
and I want to believe, Barbara,
that someone like you
will live long and merrily,
graceful and true.

Barbara, remember:
you laughed as you ran,
you ran through the rain
to be with your man,
and I walked by,
went on my way,
on through the rain.
It rained all day.

Barbara, remember:
it rained all day.
I walked round the town
and lost my way.
Two hours to kill
before my train,
and the rain came down,
the happy rain.

Pierre

I went to the café
to meet Pierre.
I went to the café,
Pierre wasn't there.
Neither was Napoleon
in that café,
but Pierre
wasn't there
in Pierre's special way.

This song summarises
Chapter 1 of Jean-
Paul Sartre *Being and
Nothingness*. Except
that where he has
(or does not have)
Wellington, we have (or
do not have) Napoleon.

Made in the USA
Charleston, SC
27 December 2010